Forming the Assembly
TO CELEBRATE
SACRAMENTS

Forming the Assembly
TO CELEBRATE SACRAMENTS

Lawrence E. Mick

LITURGY
TRAINING
PUBLICATIONS

Forming the Assembly to Celebrate Sacraments
© 2002 Archdiocese of Chicago: Liturgy Training
Publications, 1800 North Hermitage Avenue,
Chicago IL 60622-1101; 1-800-933-1800;
fax 1-800-933-7094; orders@ltp.org; www.ltp.org.
All rights reserved.

Visit our website at www.ltp.org.

This book was edited by Lorie Simmons with
assistance from Vicky Tufano. Audrey Novak Riley
was the production editor. The design is by Lucy
Smith, and the typesetting was done by Anne
Fritzinger in Minion. Printed by Sentinel Printing
Company, Inc., in St. Cloud, Minnesota. Cover photo
© Bill Wittman. Interior art by Suzanne Novak.

Library of Congress Control Number: 2002109383

ISBN 1-56854-447-2

FASAC

INTRODUCTION

This little book is about the challenge of helping people move beyond mere reform of the liturgy to a deeper sense of renewal, which was the goal sought by the Second Vatican Council when it called for liturgical reform. Reforming rites and ritual books has little value if it does not lead us to both personal and community renewal.

After the Council, much of the church's effort was devoted to creating and implementing the library of revised liturgical books to carry out the mandates of the Council. Catechesis on the changes, when it happened, focused mostly on teaching the new responses and new ritual actions that people needed to know. This was clearly a necessary stage in the liturgical reform. Simply coping with the plethora of changes that has come our way in the past decades has required a tremendous amount of energy and effort.

But we must not assume that this first stage of the reform is the only stage. Though there will be continuing revisions of the liturgical books, we do not expect in the coming years to see the number of changes that we have experienced in recent decades. Perhaps now we can turn our attention to making up for any deficiencies in catechesis that may have been inevitable in the years just after the Council.

At this moment of our history, it seems essential that we provide parishioners with the catechesis and insights they need to enter more deeply into the meaning of the liturgy. In a companion book to this volume, *Forming the Assembly to Celebrate the Mass,* I focused on how that might be done in connection with the eucharistic liturgy, our primary act of worship. In this text I want to look at the other six sacraments, to see what insights may be helpful to the people of God in enabling them to enter more deeply into these other liturgical celebrations, less frequently experienced but essential to the full Christian life.

The attention of parish leaders has commonly focused on helping people enter more fully into the celebration of Sunday Mass, which is certainly understandable since that is the primary form of liturgical celebration experienced by most Catholics. It has become apparent at occasions like weddings and funerals, however, that people do not automatically carry that deeper awareness from Sunday Mass to other liturgical situations. Coming to a wedding or the baptism of a grandchild, for example, may trigger older memories that lead people back into non-participatory stances, or some may simply be hesitant, unsure about how things are done outside their usual community.

Even when people do carry their Sunday level of participation to other occasions, they are often unaware of the profound significance of the other sacraments and thus are unable to draw deeply from the sacramental experience. Helping parishioners understand how to give themselves to these other sacramental celebrations and how the sacraments work on us will enable them to participate more vigorously and to experience more fully the rich grace of these sacraments.

This book will be an effective tool for liturgical catechesis, first with parish staff, and then with other groups in the parish. To facilitate that work, questions for reflection and discussion follow each chapter. Space has been provided after each question for the reader's notes.

The substance of this work appeared first as a series of articles in *Today's Parish* magazine. The author wishes to acknowledge the support and encouragement offered by the editor of that publication, Daniel Connors.

Chapter 1

Welcoming the Newcomer: Liturgical Formation for Baptism

In recent years we have invested much time and energy in improving the preparation of candidates for baptism. Preparation sessions for parents seeking baptism for their infants have become common in most parishes since they were mandated by the new *Rite of Infant Baptism* in 1969. The *Rite of Christian Initiation of Adults* (1972, 1988) mandated catechumenates for adults and children of catechetical age preparing for baptism, and these have now been established in most parishes. While these efforts have been of great benefit to those who have been part of these formation experiences, most parishes have been less attentive to the need for formation among the larger assembly that gathers to celebrate the initiation sacraments. Certainly celebrations of infant baptisms during Sunday Mass and celebrations of the rituals of the catechumenate have had a significant impact on all those who participate in these public rituals. Yet more can and should be done to help the average parishioner enter more fully into the celebration of initiation.

In Our Midst

Before we consider other issues, however, it is worth reflecting a bit on the importance of celebrating baptism in the midst of the parish community. Whether we are talking about infant baptism or the celebration of all the rites of the catechumenate, a fundamental point to grasp is that baptism involves the whole community. For far too long, people have thought of baptism as a largely private matter. It involved immediate family members and a couple of godparents (who were often also family members), but it did not seem important to include other members of the church community.

Yet the initiation of new members, whether they are infants, children or adults, is of vital importance to the community of faith. When a new child enters a family, by birth or by adoption, it is not only the child who is affected. Every member of the family is changed by the addition of a new member. All the members of the family have new responsibilities, enter into new relationships and find various aspects of their lives influenced by those relationships.

In a similar way, every member of the church is affected by the baptism of a new member. Those who are already part of the family of the Lord have responsibilities toward the new member, they have a relationship with the new member, and they will find their lives affected in various ways by that new relationship.

If members of the church are concerned about the future of the faith community, they will naturally rejoice when new members are added to their number. Often pastors hesitate to celebrate baptisms at Sunday Mass because some parishioners complain if the Mass takes a few minutes longer. Such complaints indicate the need for catechesis to help people understand their relationships to those being baptized. If those relationships were understood, parishioners would be disappointed *not* to be included in the celebration of baptism.

Along with the joy that should accompany the welcoming of new members, parishioners should also recognize the responsibility that is theirs. They bear a responsibility toward the newly baptized. They are called to bear witness to the new members, to share their faith with them, to guide the newly baptized into the way of Christ, to offer support in times of difficulty, to share prayer and worship and to constantly give a good example to their new brothers and sisters.

Our Shared Mission

Beyond responsibility to those who have become members of the church, every Christian also bears responsibility for the ongoing mission of the church. In speaking of the initiation of adults, the *Rite of Christian Initiation of Adults* says that this "is the responsibility of all the baptized" (#9). The church exists to bring people to Christ and to witness to God's truth and God's grace offered to all.

To properly understand baptism, members of the church must recognize that the mission of the church is entrusted to all the baptized, not just to priests and religious and full-time pastoral ministers. This is perhaps the most important catechetical point that has yet to be grasped by many Catholics. It deserves constant attention at every level of catechesis and pastoral ministry in the parish.

This is one of the basic teachings of the Second Vatican Council. The Council fathers made it clear that the whole church is the people of God. The original draft of the *Dogmatic Constitution on the Church (Lumen Gentium)* began with a chapter on the hierarchy, but the Council fathers insisted that it be changed to begin with a focus on the whole people of God. This messianic people, the Council says, is established by Christ "as a fellowship of life, charity and truth" and is "used by Him as an instrument for the redemption of all, and is sent forth into the whole world as the light of the world and the salt of the earth" (#9, in Austin Flannery, OP, ed., *Vatican Council II: The Basic Sixteen Documents* [Northport, New York: Costello, 1996]; subsequent citations are to this edition). The *Dogmatic Constitution on the Church* goes on to speak of the responsibilities that flow from being initiated into the church:

> Incorporated into the church by Baptism, the faithful are appointed by the baptismal character to christian religious worship; reborn as sons and daughters of God, they must profess publicly the faith they have received from God through the church. By the sacrament of Confirmation they are more perfectly bound to the church and are endowed with the special strength of the holy Spirit. Hence, as true witnesses of Christ, they are more strictly obliged both to spread and to defend the faith by word and by deed. (#11)

It is clear that the Council saw the work of the church as the responsibility of the whole people of God. This is a reversal of centuries of common understanding that the work of the church really belonged to the hierarchy, and that lay people were just supposed to help them when asked. In the vision of Vatican II, the work belongs to the whole church, and the hierarchy exists to help the people of God carry out their mission.

The Role of the Church in the World

Another part of the teaching of the Second Vatican Council prompts a rethinking of just what it means to be baptized. In the past, many Catholics assumed that baptism was primarily about personal salvation. Babies were to be baptized as soon as possible after birth lest they be deprived of heaven. The emphasis was on being freed from original sin and thus made worthy for eternal life.

The *Dogmatic Constitution on the Church,* however, presents a very different teaching about salvation. The Council fathers speak of salvation not only for Catholics and not only for other Christians. They also see the possibility of salvation for Jews and Muslims, for Hindus and Buddhists, and even for agnostics and atheists. Here is one sentence from the *Dogmatic Constitution on the Church:* "Nor will divine providence deny the assistance necessary for salvation to those who, without any fault of theirs, have not yet arrived at an explicit knowledge of God, and who not without grace, strive to lead a good life" (#16).

This does not reject completely the necessity of baptism. Those who have been given God's gift of faith and who recognize God's call to baptism must be baptized to be saved. To reject baptism in such a case is to reject God's will. Those who have not received the gift of faith, however, are not held accountable for what they have not received. As the gospel says, "Much will be required of the person entrusted with much, and still more will be demanded of the person entrusted with more" (Luke 12:48). Conversely, little will be required of those to whom little has been given. God judges all people on the basis of how they have responded to what they have received.

So, it still makes sense for Christian parents to have their children baptized, and it still makes sense for the church to invite others to come to faith and celebrate baptism. What is different is how we understand baptism. If people can be saved by God's grace (and we assume that millions or billions have been and are being saved), without the ritual of baptism, what does it mean when God calls some people to explicit faith in Christ and thus to baptism?

As might be expected, our understanding of the meaning of baptism is directly linked to our understanding of the identity and purpose of the church. If the church is not intended to incorporate everyone within its ranks, what is its role? Jesus himself gives us strong hints when he calls the church the leaven in the dough and the light of the world. If the dough were all leaven (yeast), it would be useless. As the role of the leaven is to raise up the whole mass of dough, so the role of the church is to raise up all of humanity. The church is to be a light to guide the world, a witness to the truth, a prophet crying out for justice, a guide to the meaning of life.

The church has pursued this role since the time of Jesus. Like the leaven in the dough, the church has always been a minority in the world (sometimes a large and powerful minority, but a minority nonetheless). Even so, that does not prevent the church from fulfilling its mission and carrying on the work of Christ.

WHY BE BAPTIZED?

So, if baptism is not primarily about personal salvation, what does it mean? If the purpose of the church is to continue the mission of Christ in the world, then those called to explicit faith in Jesus and thus to membership in the church are called to carry on that mission. They are called to baptism not simply to be a part of the company of the saved but to be a part of a community called together to carry on the work of Christ.

Thus the call to baptism is not just a call to membership in the church but a call to discipleship. Disciples of the Lord are called to carry on his work—the work of the church. Those called by God to baptism are chosen to know Christ, to live by his teaching and to give witness to his ongoing presence in the world in every age. They are called to speak the truth in season and out, to work for peace and justice, to defend the poor and the helpless, to feed the hungry and give drink to the thirsty, to do whatever helps to bring about the kingdom of God in our world.

Those who are called to baptism are God's chosen instruments. They are called to form the body of Christ in the world today so that Christ's mission of reconciling humanity to one another and to God will continue throughout the ages. Those called to baptism are not called for their own sake alone; they are called for the sake of others. A Methodist minister by the name of Harrell Beck put it this way: "The first question of Biblical religion is not 'Are you saved?' The first question of Biblical religion is 'Could God possibly use you for saving somebody else?'" ("The Jealous God of Biblical Faith vs. The Great Mush God of Public Religion," *Thesis* 1, no. 3 [1980]) That's the meaning of baptism—that God calls people to discipleship in order to save the world through their ministry.

Thus the contemporary insistence that lay people in the church have responsibility for the church's work is not simply a response to the declining number of clergy and consecrated religious. It is not something being foisted on the laity by the hierarchy. Rather it flows from the very fact of baptism. The call to ministry is an essential part of the call to baptism. Even catechumens, long before they reach the waters of the font, are expected to minister to the parish community and to share in the ministry of that community to others. An unwillingness to take on the responsibility for ministry is a clear indication that a catechumen is not ready for baptism. Those who are baptized accept responsibility for the ongoing work of the church. Church leaders direct the mission of the church, but all the baptized share in the responsibility for that mission.

Getting There

Helping parishioners grasp what is really a major shift in the church's understanding of the meaning of baptism will require consistent catechesis on all levels. This catechesis should certainly be part of the annual mystagogical preaching during the weeks of Easter. The Easter season provides a time for the whole community to reflect with the newly baptized on what it means to be baptized, to be part of the body of Christ, to be filled with the Holy Spirit and to share at the eucharistic table. Every year Easter offers a prime opportunity to deepen the assembly's understanding of their identity a bit more.

As we noted above, celebrating the rituals of the catechumenate and the baptism of infants in the midst of the parish community is a powerful form of catechesis in itself. Parish leaders should consider the best ways to make sure that all Sunday assemblies have some regular experience of the rites of initiation. Always scheduling these celebrations for the same Mass might leave the majority of the parish untouched by these formative experiences.

When the rites are celebrated, it is important for all members of the pastoral staff and worship leaders to be thoughtful about their language about initiation. If all have a clear grasp of the meaning of baptism, that will be reflected in the language of prayers, homilies and comments made to the assembly. Consistency is essential if people are going to be helped to shift their understanding of baptism.

Within the celebration of baptism, whether of adults or of infants, presiders might regularly include some opportunity for the assembly to indicate their support of those being initiated and their acceptance of responsibility to share their faith with the newly baptized. See, for example, the suggestion in #53 of the *Rite of Christian Initiation of Adults* that the presider ask both the sponsors and the assembly if they are ready to help the catechumens find and follow

Christ. Making this type of question a frequent part of parish worship can help people recognize their bonds with all who are joined to the body of Christ.

Beyond the ritual moments, parishioners need to be invited and encouraged to enter into vital relationships with those who are preparing for baptism. Most parishes that have taken the *Rite of Christian Initiation of Adults* seriously have used a variety of approaches to invite parishioners to become involved with those preparing for Christian initiation. Similar efforts might well be made for the families of infants being baptized. Consider the possibility of sponsor families who might stay in contact with the families of the newly baptized, offering assistance as well as supporting them in their responsibilities as Christian parents. Consider also ways to help the parish be aware of families expecting a child or planning to adopt—by notices in the bulletin, by special blessings at Mass for expectant parents, by prayers in the general intercessions at Mass, by pictures on the bulletin boards, and so on. Obtain the expectant parents' permission before making their news public, of course.

No one approach will suffice. The meaning of baptism is so closely linked to our identity as church that constant and consistent effort to ensure a proper understanding of this sacrament is essential to our health as a community of faith. Pastoral ministers might judge the overall effectiveness of their ministerial efforts by how well the parish comes to understand and claim their identity as the baptized.

Questions for Reflection and Discussion

1. Have you been part of the catechumenate or parent preparation sessions for infant baptism in recent years? If so, how did these experiences affect your understanding of baptism? If not, what do you know about these programs from parish announcements or talking with others?

2. Have you experienced infant or adult baptism at Mass? If so, what was your reaction? Why do you think the church encourages baptism in the midst of the parish community today?

3. How would you explain to someone the link between baptism and the call to carry on Christ's mission in the world today?

4. How do you view your own mission in the church? In what ways do you see yourself carrying on Christ's work?

5. How well do you think most Catholics understand the church's teaching about the salvation of the non-baptized? How would you explain the meaning of baptism if people can be saved without it?

6. How does calling yourself a disciple change your understanding of your role in the church and in the world?

7. What forms of catechesis do you think would be most helpful in guiding your parish to a deeper understanding of baptism?

8. Can you recall any homilies from the last Easter season in your parish? Did they help you to probe more fully the meaning of the sacraments of initiation? Did they prompt reflection on what it means to be a member of the church? Explain.

9. How central is the catechumenate to the life of your parish? How have you been involved with the catechumens and candidates for full communion? How much do you embrace your responsibility to welcome and form new members in the church community?

10. How have the rituals of the catechumenate touched you? How have they affected your understanding of baptism?

11. How could you and your parish offer more support to the parents of newly baptized infants? If you have had your own children baptized, what was helpful to you in learning how to raise them in the faith? What would have been more helpful?

Chapter 2

Rejoicing in the Spirit: Liturgical Formation for Confirmation

Of all the sacraments, perhaps none occasions more confusion in our time than the sacrament of confirmation. As Paul Turner has demonstrated clearly in his book *Confirmation: The Baby in Solomon's Court* (New York: Paulist Press, 1993), confirmation has been used and is still being used in the Catholic church for a variety of purposes and in a variety of contexts.

Though most Catholics think of confirmation as the sacrament that confers the gift of the Holy Spirit, the church also uses confirmation to incorporate Christians from other denominations into full communion with the Catholic church. This suggests the ancient use of the sacrament to celebrate the reconciliation of heretics, though the current language of the rites for coming into full communion does not speak of such people as heretical.

The more familiar source of confusion about the sacrament is the varying order in which the sacraments of initiation are received. Those baptized as Catholics in infancy celebrate confirmation later in life, often years after first communion. Children of catechetical age who enter the church through the catechumenate, on the other hand, celebrate baptism, confirmation and first communion in the same ceremony and in that order, as do adults who enter through the catechumenate.

Some parishes and some dioceses have begun to celebrate confirmation before first communion for children baptized as Catholics in their infancy. Though this does not provide one integrated celebration of initiation, it does restore the traditional order of these three sacraments.

Less well known to most parishioners is the fact that infant confirmation has a long history in the church and is still common among the Eastern rites of the church and among Spanish-speaking Catholics.

Pick an Age

Even noting this variety in the ways we celebrate confirmation should make it obvious that confirmation is not about reaching a certain age. For many Catholics, however, their concept of this sacrament is closely tied to a notion of Christian maturity. Often parish or diocesan policies reinforce this misunderstanding by requiring that children must reach a certain age before they can be confirmed. While there may be pastoral reasons for such decisions (as well as the fact that current canon law links the sacrament to the "age of reason"), it is important that our catechesis be guided by the fundamental meaning of the sacrament.

Our understanding of that meaning, which was shaped by the medieval understanding of this sacrament for so long, has been significantly revised as a result of modern liturgical scholarship. We now have access to documents of the early church that were unavailable to medieval theologians. The discovery of these documents has helped us recover the ancient understanding of this sacrament, leading to the renewal of the sacrament mandated by the Second Vatican Council.

We need to be clear: Confirmation is not about puberty, adolescence or any other stage of human maturity. The basic mandate of the Council in reforming this sacrament was to make clear its intimate connection with baptism. For much of our history as a church, the anointing of confirmation was celebrated in the same ceremony as the water bath of baptism. What later was separated into two sacraments was once an integral rite of initiation into the life of the church. That integral celebration has been restored for both adults and children of catechetical age in the *Rite of Christian Initiation of Adults*.

The close connection between baptism and confirmation means that our understanding of confirmation must stay very close to our understanding of baptism. It is only a slight exaggeration to say that whatever we can say about confirmation we can also say about baptism. A person who is ready for baptism is, theologically speaking, also ready for confirmation.

At this point in our history, then, we could pick almost any age for confirmation and justify it. How candidates experience the celebration of the sacrament will obviously vary according to their age and background, just as with baptism. God deals with us according to our age and abilities. Just as more is required of an adult preparing for baptism than is required of an infant to be baptized, so what is required for confirmation will vary according to the abilities of those to be confirmed. The issue is not really a question of the proper age. The issue is how we initiate people of any age into the community of faith.

THE SPIRIT WE SHARE

Rather than celebrating the attainment of a certain age or some stage of maturity, confirmation celebrates the gift of the Holy Spirit that is shared in the faith community. This Spirit is given in baptism (which is why confirmation is so closely linked with baptism), so if we are confirming children who were baptized years earlier, it is not a question of conferring the Spirit upon people who do not already have this gift. They already have the Spirit dwelling in them.

Understanding the significance of confirmation is easier if we consider it in the context of the integral celebration of the three sacraments of initiation. In that celebration, the water bath of baptism focuses our attention on incorporation into the death and resurrection of Christ. The anointing we call confirmation focuses our attention on the gift of the Spirit, who brings about that incorporation into Christ. The eucharist focuses our attention on our identity as members of the body of Christ and as disciples called to carry on the mission of the Lord. All three of these sacraments express and celebrate different aspects of our initiation into Christ's body.

The purpose of confirmation, then, is to celebrate the gift of the Spirit that is an integral aspect of our life in Christ. This Spirit is given to all members of the community and is the glue that binds us into one body. If we are truly a community of faith, then we live by the power of and under the guidance of the Holy Spirit. When the community gathers around those who are to be confirmed, the assembly is celebrating the presence of the Holy Spirit in the community of the church. That celebration focuses on the presence of the Spirit in the lives of those being confirmed, as that Spirit has been revealed in their attitudes and their actions.

This basic reality of the church celebrating the presence of the Holy Spirit applies regardless of the age of those being confirmed. If the one seeking confirmation is an adult, we celebrate the Spirit as that Spirit is revealed in the life of that adult. If the person is an infant, we celebrate the Spirit's presence in the believing family, just as we celebrate the family's faith in infant baptism. If those being confirmed are children (of whatever age) we celebrate the presence of the Spirit in their lives, revealed in ways appropriate to their age.

THE COMMUNITY'S ROLE

The challenge for formation of the assembly, of course, is that many of them do not recognize what they are celebrating or even that their role is central to the celebration. People still tend to think of sacraments primarily in terms of what happens to the recipients. Consistent catechesis is needed to help them recognize that every sacrament is a celebration by the whole assembly gathered in faith.

If the community is going to be able to celebrate the presence of the Spirit in their midst, in themselves as well as in the candidates for confirmation, many of them will need to grow in their own awareness of the Spirit in their own lives. It is no secret that the Western Christian churches have paid less attention to the Spirit than have the churches of the East. The celebration of confirmation in a parish provides an opportunity to address that deficiency periodically.

Formation of the whole parish might well parallel the formation of the candidates. Parishioners should be challenged to examine their own awareness of and response to the Spirit in their lives. Do they listen for the voice of the Spirit? Do they rely on the Spirit's guidance when they confront significant decisions? Do they call upon the Spirit's strength when they face difficult situations? Do they try to manifest the gifts of the Holy Spirit in their lives? Can they name the gifts of the Spirit? Our tradition speaks of seven gifts and twelve fruits of the Spirit. Is that tradition a living one in the parish? Do people seek to shape their lives in a way that enables those gifts to bear such fruit?

Beyond such issues, which relate to one's personal attention to and response to the Spirit, the community might also be challenged to examine how the parish itself reflects the presence and guidance of the Holy Spirit. Sometimes parish meetings and organizations seem to manifest a very different spirit! It may be a spirit of dissension and division rather than the Spirit of unity. It may be a spirit of self-interest and competition rather than the Spirit of self-giving and cooperation. It may even be a spirit of hatred and condemnation rather than the Spirit of love and encouragement. How could such a community honestly celebrate the gift of the Holy Spirit if its members were not willing to live by that same Spirit in their dealings with one another? In such a case it might be appropriate for the bishop to delay celebrating confirmation until the parish embraced reconciliation and learned to live in the Spirit!

As parishioners examine their own behavior and attentiveness to the Spirit, they might also be encouraged to notice signs of the Spirit's presence and action in the lives of all those preparing for confirmation. This presumes, of course, that the parish community knows who those candidates are. If this is not normally the case, making the candidates known and linking them in various ways to other members of the parish might be the best place to begin. Sacraments rarely become true community celebrations if the community does not have some relationship with the candidates for that sacrament.

The Community and the Candidates

Beyond simply having a relationship with those to be confirmed, the community should also be involved in the formation and preparation of the candidates. The whole process is a time for the community to draw the candidates into its way of life, a life based on the power of the Spirit. If the community is truly living in the Spirit, then it will be able to invite its young people (or adults in the catechumenate) to enter into that communal life. As the candidates gradually learn to live more fully in the Spirit, the community's life and witness are enriched and strengthened. It is this growing involvement of the candidates in the life of the faith community that gives the community reason to celebrate.

It should be clear by this point that this perspective on confirmation focuses first on the community's celebration and the reasons it has to celebrate. All the sacraments celebrate the presence and action of God already at work in the lives of the candidates and in the community as a whole. The first question about a sacrament should not be what is happening to the candidates but what the community is celebrating around these candidates.

This does not mean that the sacraments have no effect, however. Celebrating the reality of God's action in our lives has an effect both on the community and on the candidates who form the focus of the celebration. Celebrating almost anything reinforces the importance and power of that reality in our lives. When a married couple celebrates an anniversary, the very act of celebrating reinforces their commitment to one another. When they share that anniversary celebration with others, the celebration also reinforces the commitment of other married couples and even the commitment of unmarried people to be faithful to the relationships in their own lives.

In a similar way, when the community celebrates the gift of the Spirit that they have seen revealed in the lives of the candidates, that celebration reinforces both the awareness of the Spirit and the power of the Spirit in the lives of the candidates. At the same time, it reinforces that same awareness and power in the lives of all those who take part in the celebration.

Seeing confirmation in this way differs greatly from seeing it simply as a milestone in the maturation of a young boy or girl. Extensive catechesis is needed if the assembly is to take its proper role in the celebration of confirmation in the parish. The periodic celebration of this sacrament in any faith community is a rich opportunity for the whole parish to grow in its spiritual life. It is not an accident that we speak of the *spiritual* life of a community of faith. That life is shaped by, guided by, powered by and sustained by the Spirit that is given to each of us when we are initiated into the church community. If the community is to become more spiritually alive, it will do so only to the extent that it learns to respond more fully to the voice of the Spirit within it. Such an energized and enlivened community of faith is both the challenge and the promise of confirmation. Efforts to form the whole community to celebrate the sacrament well will pay rich dividends for all areas of the parish's mission and ministry.

QUESTIONS FOR REFLECTION AND DISCUSSION

1. What do you remember about your own confirmation? How did you understand its meaning at the time? How do you understand it now?

2. How would you explain to someone why we have two different patterns for the reception of the initiation sacraments at this point in our history?

3. How would you respond to someone who asks you, "What is the proper age for confirmation?"

4. If confirmation is not a "sacrament of maturity," how else might the church work with teenagers to help them personally embrace the faith into which they were baptized?

5. What role does the Holy Spirit play in your personal spiritual life? How aware of the Spirit is your parish community? What would be effective in increasing that awareness?

6. If the Holy Spirit is given to us in baptism, how would you explain the purpose of the sacrament of confirmation?

7. To what degree is your parish community involved in the preparation of candidates for confirmation? How could greater involvement be fostered?

8. Does the community seek to discern awareness and action of the Holy Spirit in the lives of candidates for confirmation? Is readiness determined for each candidate or is it assumed that all members of a certain class will automatically be confirmed? Which do you think is more appropriate and why?

9. How would you describe the effects of confirmation on those confirmed? On the parish community?

10. How well do you think your parish celebrates confirmation? Is it truly a community-wide event? How could more people be drawn into the celebration?

Chapter 3

Celebrating God's Mercy: Liturgical Formation for Penance

The *Constitution on the Sacred Liturgy* of the Second Vatican Council decreed: "The rite and formularies for the sacrament of penance are to be revised so that they more clearly express both the nature and effect of the sacrament" (#72, in *The Liturgy Documents: A Parish Resource,* vol. 1 [Chicago: Liturgy Training Publications, 1991]; subsequent references to this document are to this edition). That is the only sentence about this sacrament in the conciliar document, but it led to a major reform of the rituals of penance, issued from Rome in 1973.

If the hope of those who created the new rituals was a renewed appreciation for and use of this sacrament (as it surely was), they must be disappointed with the results thus far. The new rite apparently did little to stem the precipitous decline in the use of this sacrament.

Many Catholics seem to have abandoned it completely, while others make much less use of it than before. Moreover, even the implementation of the rituals themselves seems spotty at best, with many Catholics still approaching the sacrament as they did before the Council. In the individual form of penance, elements that should be standard are often omitted. In the communal form, a variety of practices have developed, some of which seem more focused on efficiency than on deepening the experience of God's forgiving love.

Certainly some Catholics have renewed their understanding of penance and have grown spiritually through healthy use of this opportunity for reconciliation and ongoing conversion. Their numbers, however, clearly constitute a minority of the Catholic population. More catechesis and formation are still needed.

A Broad Perspective

When we consider what kind of formation and catechesis is necessary for people to enter deeply into this sacrament, a broad focus is essential. The issues often go far beyond the realm of the sacrament itself. Penance is also called the sacrament of reconciliation, and reconciliation assumes an awareness of alienation that needs healing.

Surveys over recent decades have often noted that one reason for declining use of the sacrament of penance is a change in people's sense of sin. This does not seem to be simply an abandonment of responsibility for one's actions. It flows in part from an awareness of psychological factors that affect one's freedom and thus one's degree of responsibility. It is also partly a reaction to preconciliar moral teaching that seemed very black and white without much room for the gray. It rejects a culture of guilt that was often used to ensure proper behavior in past generations. Finally, it is linked to a broader awareness of social sin and structural sin, which are more difficult to judge in terms of one's personal responsibility.

Formation for celebrating the sacrament of penance, therefore, must include solid formation in questions of conscience, moral norms, the reality of sin and the necessity of acknowledging one's own sinfulness. This is a vast challenge, of course, and one that must be addressed at every level of catechetical instruction. Beyond formal catechetical classes, parishes might work with parents to help them catechize their own children in matters of morality, sin, repentance and forgiveness. This might include pointers for parents who are helping their young children prepare for first confession, guidance for parents who are supporting their middle-grade children as they develop their moral awareness, and sessions for parents who are facing great difficulties in finding a balance between guiding their teens in moral behavior and nurturing their growth into independence.

Perhaps it is also time to consider whether preachers have steered a bit too clear of morality in homilies. While a homily should not moralize in the sense of simply telling people what to do and what not to do, the scriptures offer ample material for the formation of conscience according to gospel values. Preachers need to find ways to challenge people to repentance and conversion without oversimplifying moral issues.

A Forgiving God

Some people claim that the loss of a sense of sin is a result of the postconciliar emphasis on the love of God. Our changing image of God from a judge to be feared to a deity who loves without limit certainly affects our understanding of sin. But a true image of a loving God should heighten our sense of sin, for all sin is a rejection of that immense love.

That we have the ability and even proclivity to reject such marvelous love is the conundrum of human existence. Yet we do it. And the message of the gospel is not that a loving God doesn't care about our sins but that this God is willing to forgive us whenever we turn back to embrace God's love.

The issue might be simplified in these terms. Before the Council we thought of ourselves as corrupt; after the Council we have tended to think of ourselves as sinless. The truth is that we are sinful but we are also forgiven. As one bumper sticker puts it: "Christians are not perfect; they're just forgiven."

That slogan perhaps sums up the two fundamental points of catechesis that are needed today: Christians are imperfect sinners, and God is a forgiving God. It is these two truths that form the basis for celebrating the sacrament of penance.

Understanding the Rituals

Beyond this broader catechesis, there is also need to help people to understand both the shape and the purposes of the different forms of penance available today. Though the designers of the new rite of penance envisioned three forms, Vatican restrictions on the use of the third form with general absolution make it a rarity.

The two forms that are commonly available to parishioners are the individual form and a communal penance service that includes individual confession and absolution. Pastoral experience suggests that there is need for ongoing catechesis about each of these ways of celebrating the sacrament of reconciliation.

The Individual Form

When the transition to the new rite was in process in 1973, it was common to hear the individual form of reconciliation described as basically the same as the preconciliar experience of the sacrament. There was some new language, and face-to-face confession soon became an option in most places, but people were encouraged to think of this form of the sacrament as simply a minor updating of what they had always known.

In fact, however, the changes in this ritual are far more than cosmetic. What is fundamentally different is the overall atmosphere of the rite. The experience before the council was primarily cast in judicial images. The confessor was the judge, and the penitent was both prosecutor and defendant. The penitent had to make a complete confession so that the confessor would know what punishment to assign as a penance. The experience was generally in a dark and confined space, a largely impersonal encounter through a screen with anonymity as a high value.

The new rite, by contrast, is envisioned as a time of shared prayer between penitent and confessor. Less a judge than a spiritual doctor, the confessor seeks to understand the person's spiritual condition, to give helpful guidance and to assign a penance that will assist in healing the penitent's spiritual illness. The encounter is more personal, with welcoming words at the beginning, a space that is well-lit and pleasant and the option of speaking face-to-face. The rite is intended to conclude with words of praise to God for the gift of forgiveness and healing.

Many people, however, have not grasped this new approach very well. Those who come to individual confession often begin as they did years ago, allowing no opportunity for words of welcome or the proclamation of scripture that is supposed to precede one's confession of sins. The face-to-face option is still foreign to many, and any real dialogue with the penitent is stymied by an approach that aims for minimal self-revelation in a sterile ritual.

There is need, then, to catechize broadly about the manner of celebrating reconciliation in its individual form. Many younger Catholics do not carry the baggage of the past, but often their only experience of the sacrament has been in the communal form. They need to be equipped to use the individual form when that is helpful for their spiritual growth.

The Communal Penance Service

Perhaps the most successful part of the reform of this sacrament has been the use of the communal form with individual confession on a regular basis in most parishes, most commonly in Advent and Lent. Those who participate seem to grasp, at least to some degree, the communal nature of our sin and of reconciliation. This is probably the way that most Catholics in the United States experience the sacrament today.

Given this fact, it seems doubly important to make sure that this experience is a rich and full one. Sometimes the press of numbers influences pastoral leaders to aim for efficiency above all else. Some pastors tell penitents to confess only one sin rather than making a complete confession. Some designate a common penance (usually some prayer said jointly) rather than tailoring individual penances to the conversion journey of the penitents. Some even omit part of the formula of absolution, reducing it to a juridical statement rather than a prayer text.

Certainly the declining number of presbyters sometimes makes it difficult to gather sufficient priests to allow a reasonable time with each penitent. More often, however, it seems that pastors resort to these approaches because they do not allow enough opportunities for reconciliation. In a large parish, for example, several communal services during Lent make more sense than trying to provide for all penitents in one hour.

On the other hand, people do need to recognize that the communal form does provide only a brief time for dialogue with a confessor. This is not the time for long discussions of one's spiritual state. People need to be helped to understand the different values inherent in the individual form and the communal service so that they can choose the form that best suits their needs at a given time.

THE ELEMENTS OF RECONCILIATION

An element of catechesis that is often very helpful to people is a brief history of the sacrament of penance. Even a quick overview indicates how much this sacrament has varied in its form and usage through the centuries.

Through all its variations, however, one can discern three elements that seem to be common: confession of sin, doing the penance, and absolution or reconciliation. Though they have been celebrated in different order (confession, penance, reconciliation in the early centuries; confession, absolution, penance after the 8th century; absolution, penance, confession within a year with general absolution), all three elements are generally retained. Each of these elements has been dominant in people's awareness at different times, and the sacrament has accordingly been called confession, penance or reconciliation in different eras.

Basic catechesis about the sacrament can revolve around these three crucial elements. Helping parishioners to understand the purpose and nature of each of the elements will prepare them to enter more deeply into the meaning and power of this sacrament.

Confession
The importance of a "good confession" can hardly be overemphasized. The crucial question is what we mean by "good." The act of

confession on the part of the penitent is ultimately an act of self-revelation. It is not so much a matter of making sure that every sin is confessed (that is only required for serious or mortal sins) but of making sure that one conveys the true nature of one's spiritual condition. Though the focus is on the spiritual illness that needs to be healed, it is also sometimes appropriate to tell the confessor some of the positive elements of one's spiritual life in order to communicate a balanced and accurate perspective.

The challenge for most of us is to get below the surface of our sinful actions and to discover and then reveal the true source of those actions. Sometimes the confessor can help the penitent make such a discovery, but a good examination of conscience may also lead to such insight. Teaching people how to examine their lives should include not only how to recognize sinful actions but also how to search their hearts for the attitudes and desires that lead them into sin. This is an important part of formation for proper celebration of the sacrament of penance.

Penance

It is in light of such insights into the sources of sinful actions that the role of the penance within the sacrament makes sense. In the early centuries of the church, the whole process of reconciliation was modeled on the catechumenate. Both were designed to bring about conversion of one's life to Christ. The penance, often carried out over a substantial period of time, was to foster such conversion. Only after true conversion was evident did it make sense to celebrate reconciliation or absolution.

In later centuries, absolution is given at the time of confession contingent on the promise that the penitent will do the penance afterward. The goal of the penance is still the same, however—to foster conversion. A good confessor listens carefully to what the penitent reveals about his or her life and then tries to assign a penance that will help the person to take the next step on the road of conversion. Penitents need to recognize the value of a good penance in fostering their own spiritual growth and take seriously whatever guidance the confessor offers to promote such progress in the spiritual journey.

Reconciliation

The first two elements of the sacrament, that is, making a good confession and performing the assigned penance, are largely the work of the penitent. What is more important, however, is the work of God—reconciliation. Efforts to emphasize God's activity in the sacrament are reflected in the contemporary practice of calling this the sacrament of reconciliation. It is God's forgiving love that is the basis of the celebration—we hardly have reason to celebrate our sins! What we celebrate is the grace of God that enables us to repent and begin again, the incredible love of God that forgives us no matter how seriously we have sinned. Though much progress has been made since the Council in helping people recognize our God as a loving God, there is ongoing need for solid preaching and catechesis that will enable parishioners to be drawn toward that love. Ultimately it is the recognition of God's immense love that will lead people to risk self-revelation in order to rejoice in God's amazing forgiveness.

SOME PRACTICAL POINTERS

There are numerous practical suggestions that can be offered to parishioners to help them enter more fully into the celebration of this sacrament. These might be topics addressed periodically in the bulletin, in homilies and in religious education.

Remind penitents, especially for individual confession, that the rite begins with the sign of the cross. This simple text and gesture can help them remember that the sacrament is shared prayer rather than a courtroom judgment.

Penitents might be encouraged to choose a scripture reading for use during the celebration of individual reconciliation. Most confessors would probably welcome such initiative, and the very process of deciding what passage is appropriate can be part of the penitent's discovery of what really needs to happen for conversion to be advanced.

Penitents might also be invited to suggest what penance might be best for themselves. Again, most confessors would probably welcome such suggestions, and deciding what one needs to do to further one's own conversion will already give an impetus to that process.

Consider teaching parishioners the ritual exchange in the individual rite after the absolution. The confessor says, "Give thanks to the Lord, for he is good." The penitent responds, "His mercy endures forever." This simple exchange can remind penitents that the core of the sacrament is God's loving forgiveness rather than their sinfulness.

Conclusion

The current state of the sacrament of penance is the result of many years and even centuries of teaching and practice. It will take much effort over a long time to recover a healthy understanding and use of this sacrament. Such effort, however, can lead us to a time when Christians once again know the power and the joy of encountering a forgiving God who wipes away our tears and leads us to newness of life.

Questions for Reflection and Discussion

1. Describe your use of the sacrament of penance over your lifetime. Has it changed in frequency, in style, in what you discuss? How has your understanding of the sacrament changed?

2. How has your understanding of sin changed since you were a child? How has that affected your use of this sacrament?

3. How much catechesis on sin and morality is offered in your parish? Do you think it is adequate for children and for adults? What forms of catechesis might be effective in your community?

4. Describe the last homily you can recall that dealt with a moral issue. Was it clearly based on the readings or the feast of the day? How helpful was it to you?

5. How has your image of God changed over your lifetime? How has this affected your understanding of sin?

6. Can you explain the purpose of the two different forms of penance in common use today? Do you use both forms at times? How do you decide which form to celebrate?

7. What did this chapter teach you or remind you about the individual form of the sacrament? Describe your own experience with this form.

8. What did this chapter teach you or remind you about communal penance services? Describe several different communal services you have experienced, if you can.

9. How would you explain the meaning of a "good confession" within the sacrament? How has your understanding of this changed?

10. Recall some penances that you have been given in the sacrament. How have they helped you to change your life?

11. What differences do you see in calling this the "sacrament of reconciliation" rather than the "sacrament of penance"? Which term do you prefer and why?

Chapter 4

Embracing the Sick:
Liturgical Formation
for Anointing

When I was ordained in 1972 and began parish ministry, I soon became aware of the fear that gripped people when I would arrive at a home or hospital to administer extreme unction. The renewed rite for the sacrament of the anointing of the sick was issued from Rome at the end of that year, but it took a while for the significance of the reform of this sacrament to be grasped by the faithful. For a long time many Catholics retained a pre–Vatican II understanding of the anointing. Thinking of it as extreme unction, they saw the arrival of the priest as the kiss of death. Even though the church had changed the sacrament's name and offered it to anyone who was seriously ill, pastoral ministers had to discern carefully whether offering this sacrament would console or terrify the patient and his or her family.

This pastoral situation was not surprising, for the shift in perspective on this sacrament after the Second Vatican Council was a profound one. Learning to see the sacrament as a source of healing for the sick instead of the final act of the church before a person died required a significant change in both thought and emotional responses on the part of the Catholic faithful.

Much progress has been made since those days. The majority of active Catholics today recognize that the anointing is intended for the sick, not just for the dying. Most are quite willing to request the anointing for themselves or their loved ones when they face serious illness. Of course, there are many inactive Catholics who have not made this transition in perspective yet. Having little or no contact with the church until a time of crisis, they will often call parishes to request "the last rites" for a dying family member with no awareness that anything has changed.

Even among many Catholics who are active, however, the shift in understanding of this sacrament is far from complete. Continuing formation is needed to help them to better understand the meaning and proper use of the anointing of the sick.

CARE OF THE SICK

One crucial step in this continuing formation is to see the anointing as part of a broader pattern of pastoral care of the sick. It is no accident that the current U.S. ritual book for this sacrament is titled *Pastoral Care of the Sick: Rites of Anointing and Viaticum.* The title is intended to remind us that the anointing is only one of the ways that the church cares for the sick and that it is best celebrated in the context of ongoing pastoral care of those experiencing serious illness.

The rite itself puts it this way: "It is thus especially fitting that all baptized Christians share in this ministry of mutual charity within the Body of Christ by doing all that they can to help the sick return to health, by showing love for the sick, and by celebrating the sacraments with them. Like the other sacraments, these too have a community aspect, which should be brought out as much as possible when they are celebrated" (#33, in *Pastoral Care of the Sick/Cuidado Pastoral de los Enfermos* [Chicago: Liturgy Training Publications, 1986]; subsequent references are to this edition).

The text goes on to note that the family and friends of the sick and those who take care of them have a special share in this ministry. They are encouraged to share words of faith with the sick, to pray with them and to encourage them to link their suffering with the passion and death of Christ. If the sickness grows worse, then they should contact the pastor and prepare for the celebration of the sacrament.

Many Catholics do not see the sacrament in this broader context. Too often they wait until a loved one is at a point of crisis before they even let the church know that the person is dealing with a serious illness. Many parishes today have a "network of care" or other group of pastoral ministers who seek to provide a wide range of services for the sick. Encouraging parishioners to call upon such services can help them move past the crisis approach. Ongoing pastoral care provides a context in which the celebration of the sacrament of the sick can find a natural place.

GATHER THE CHURCH

Just as the overall care of the sick should involve other members of the parish, so the celebration of the sacrament of anointing also calls for the participation of other parishioners. Ideally, the anointing of the sick is celebrated in the midst of a gathering of the church around the sick person. This is perhaps the key area that needs further catechesis today.

Like all sacraments, as the quotation above reminds us, the anointing of the sick is a celebration of the church community. The members of the church gather around the sick person(s) to offer the support of a shared faith and shared prayer. The priest presides, as he does normally when the church gathers for worship, but it is the whole gathered community that celebrates the sacrament with him around the sick person(s).

The size of the gathered community will vary according to the circumstances in each situation. Sometimes it will be a full assembly, as when the anointing is celebrated at a parish Mass for all those who are able to come to the church despite their illnesses. Such a celebration would normally include song and communal prayer as the context for the anointing, and it most often will take place during the celebration of the eucharist. This might be a special Mass, or it might be one of the regular Sunday celebrations of the parish.

Sometimes the assembly will be a smaller group at the church, as when someone requests anointing before entering the hospital for major surgery. In many parishes today, such a person would be anointed during a daily Mass, so that the gathered community is made up of those who come to Mass that day. It might also be done in connection with a gathering for Morning Prayer or Evening Prayer in the parish.

Sometimes the assembly may be even smaller, as is common when someone is anointed in a hospital setting. It may be only members of the family who gather for the celebration of the sacrament, though it is desirable even in such situations that some other members of the parish be called to join them to offer support and shared faith.

There will also be times, of course, when an emergency requires celebrating the sacrament with only the priest and the sick person present. Such a celebration is still a valid sacrament, yet it should be the exception rather than the rule.

The issue here, as with all the sacraments, is that the celebration of a sacrament is supposed to take place in the midst of, and with the involvement of, an assembly of believers. As the *Constitution on the Sacred Liturgy* reminds us, "Whenever rites, according to their specific nature, make provision for communal celebration involving the presence and active participation of the faithful, it is to be stressed that this way of celebrating them is to be preferred, as far as possible, to a celebration that is individual and, so to speak, private" (#27). Many Catholics still do not recognize that this principle applies to the anointing of the sick as well as to all other sacramental celebrations.

REACHING OUT

Those requesting anointing for their loved ones need to understand this perspective. Too often people request an anointing for a sick person but see no reason to be present when it is celebrated. It is still sometimes seen as a quasi-magical act that only needs to be performed to cause its effects. A full and rich celebration by an assembly gathered around a sick person is much more likely to be spiritually fruitful than a minimal celebration with only the priest and the patient.

Beyond the need for family members and friends of the sick person to understand the importance of gathering an assembly of Christians for the celebration, it is important for the whole parish to understand their responsibilities toward the sick and the dying members of the community. Many parishes have a dedicated group of parishioners who offer support to families at the time of a funeral. Sometimes this involves simply preparing a meal for the mourners after the funeral itself. Often it is much more extensive, providing meals throughout the time of preparing for the funeral and beyond, house-sitting during the funeral itself, visiting in the weeks and months following the funeral, and so on.

Some parishes have another group similarly dedicated to the care of the sick. They provide continuing contact in the name of the parish with those who are living with long-term illnesses, especially those who are homebound or hospitalized. They seek to meet a variety of needs including social visiting, providing meals, offering caregivers a respite, sharing prayer and bringing communion. Because they develop a significant relationship, they are in a position to help the pastor know when it seems appropriate to offer other sacramental ministry, whether reconciliation or anointing of the sick or viaticum at the time of death.

ANOINTING OR VIATICUM?

A major point of confusion that needs to be addressed is what sacrament is appropriate at what stage. The old understanding of the anointing as extreme unction still leads many people, including some pastoral ministers, to link the anointing with the moment of death.

The current rite, on the other hand, embodies a very different perspective. The appropriate recipients for the anointing of the sick are described in the general introduction of the rite:

> Great care and concern should be taken to see that those of
> the faithful whose health is seriously impaired by sickness
> or old age receive this sacrament.

A prudent or reasonably sure judgment, without scruple, is sufficient for deciding on the seriousness of an illness; if necessary a doctor may be consulted.

The sacrament may be repeated if the sick person recovers after being anointed and then again falls ill or if during the same illness the person's condition becomes more serious.

A sick person may be anointed before surgery whenever a serious illness is the reason for the surgery.

Elderly people may be anointed if they have become notably weakened even though no serious illness is present.

Sick children are to be anointed if they have sufficient use of reason to be strengthened by this sacrament. In a case of doubt whether a child has reached the use of reason, the sacrament is to be conferred. (#8–12)

This listing makes it clear that the anointing is intended for all who are seriously ill, not just for the dying. The proper sacrament for the dying is not the anointing but viaticum, or communion for the dying. The rite notes that "All baptized Christians who are able to receive communion are bound to receive viaticum by reason of the precept to receive communion when in danger of death from any cause" (#27). Though normally given by the parish priest, viaticum may be given by any priest or deacon, "or if no ordained minister is available, any member of the faithful who has been duly appointed" (#29).

Viaticum is food for the journey, intended to accompany Christians in their passage from this life to the next. When possible, the rite notes, viaticum should be received within Mass and given under both kinds. Though this is the sacrament for the dying, the rite insists that "priests with pastoral responsibility must see that the celebration of this sacrament is not delayed, but that the faithful are nourished by it while still in full possession of their faculties" (#27).

Of course, there will be situations where people have no advance warning of the need for anointing or viaticum. In such cases, the rite provides for celebrating penance, anointing and viaticum in a single celebration. It notes, additionally, that if there is not enough time for all three sacraments, penance and viaticum are to be celebrated first; then the person may be anointed, if there is sufficient time (#30).

Ongoing Catechesis

Helping the faithful understand when to ask for which sacrament is, in itself, a challenge that requires long-term catechesis. We might almost consider bumper stickers that read "Anointing for the sick, viaticum for the dying." Getting that principle firmly in the minds of the church as a whole would be a major step forward.

Sometimes people want their loved one anointed even after they have died. The rite is very clear that anointing is not to be given to someone who is already dead. "Instead, he [the priest] should pray for them, asking that God forgive their sins and graciously receive them into the kingdom"(#15). Sacraments can only be celebrated with the living; those who have died have gone beyond the realm of sacraments. If there is doubt whether the person is actually dead, then the anointing should be celebrated, using the shortened rite provided for emergencies.

Continuing catechesis is also needed to help people understand the communal nature of the anointing (and of all sacraments) and their broader responsibilities to offer support and assistance to the sick members of the faith community.

The rite itself notes the necessity of catechesis of the faithful: "It is important that all the faithful, and above all the sick, be aided by suitable catechesis in preparing for and participating in the sacraments of anointing and viaticum, especially if the celebration is to be carried out communally" (#36).

This sacrament is an important ministry that the church can offer its members in times of great difficulty. It can be a powerful witness of God's love and a welcome support for suffering members of the body of Christ. Helping parishioners understand this sacrament more deeply will enable them to take full advantage of the riches it has to offer.

QUESTIONS FOR REFLECTION AND DISCUSSION

1. How has your understanding of the anointing of the sick changed over the years?

2. Recall any times that you have experienced this sacrament, whether as a patient or as a member of the community present for someone else's anointing. What parts of the rite struck you most powerfully?

3. How does your parish care for the spiritual needs of its members who are sick? Who provides this care? In what ways does the parish meet the various needs of the sick?

4. If you were seriously ill or facing major surgery, would you request the anointing for yourself? Why or why not?

5. How would you explain to someone when the anointing of the sick should be celebrated?

6. How could your parish involve more parishioners in the celebration of this sacrament? What would it take for the parish to reach the point that those anointed by your priest(s) are normally surrounded by members of the parish?

7. How would you explain to a neighbor or a relative the meaning of viaticum and the appropriate time to celebrate it?

8. Who are the proper candidates for the anointing of the sick?

9. How would you explain why the church does not anoint those who have already died?

10. How would you describe the purpose and value of the sacrament of anointing?

Chapter 5

Calling Forth Church Leaders: Liturgical Formation for Holy Orders

O f all seven sacraments, the one least familiar to most Catholics is the sacrament of holy orders. The reason for this is simple— it is the sacrament that is celebrated the least often. Even in years past when large numbers of priests were ordained each year in many dioceses, those ordinations commonly took place in one ceremony at one place, the diocesan cathedral. Family members and friends of those being ordained would travel to the cathedral for the celebration, but others would not. Most Catholics have never been present for an ordination.

This remains true even though the number of ordination Masses has increased somewhat, due to the restoration of the diaconate. Ordination Masses for permanent deacons have taken place in most dioceses in recent decades. There was some movement in the 1970s and 1980s in some dioceses to celebrate ordinations in the home parishes of those being ordained, but this pattern did not become widespread. Even where it is the custom, the decrease in the numbers of those being ordained as priests still makes the celebration of holy orders rather rare.

INFREQUENT YET ESSENTIAL

At the same time, the sacrament of holy orders is essential to every member of the church. Without this sacrament, there would be no eucharist, no sacrament of penance, no anointing of the sick and ultimately no church. The essential nature of this sacrament for the ongoing life of the church community makes it important for all members of the assembly to understand and appreciate it.

This presents parish leaders with a dilemma. It might logically be argued that preparing the parish to celebrate the sacrament of orders is futile if most parishioners never experience such a celebration. It is difficult to effectively catechize people on a matter that they do not see as an imminent concern. Yet some parishioners will experience ordinations and need to know how to participate. Moreover, even those who never take part in an actual celebration of this sacrament need to understand it and its role in the life of the church.

One possible approach, of course, is to encourage parishioners to take part in ordinations. Whenever a diocese ordains new priests or deacons or a new bishop, it is appropriate for the assembly for that celebration to include members of every parish in the diocese. Arranging for at least some members of each parish to take part in such celebrations provides a natural opportunity for catechizing the parish as a whole about the significance of holy orders for the whole community of faith. Such participation and the accompanying catechesis of the parish may also be one of the more effective approaches to encouraging more vocations to ordained ministry.

THE COMMUNITY CONNECTION

One basic insight that people need in order to properly understand this sacrament is that ordination is less about a conferral of powers than it is about entering an order dedicated to the service of the Christian community. On a practical level, many Catholics have not begun to understand this shift in perspective about holy orders that has developed after the Second Vatican Council.

This shift, like most developments following the Council, is really a return to our early tradition. In the early centuries of church history, it was clear that people were ordained to serve the needs of the local church community. Those to be ordained were chosen from (and often by) the local community because they were recognized as leaders in the community. They were chosen because the community had a need for leadership. The different orders that have existed within the church in various centuries all developed to meet particular needs of the church at particular times.

In our own time, there has been considerable effort to reestablish the link between the ordained and the local church community. While local communities do not choose their own leaders to be ordained as priests and most pastors are appointed from outside the local parish, priests have learned to see their identity as more closely linked to the communities they serve. Moreover, permanent deacons are often leaders in their parishes before they are ordained, and many return to those parishes to serve the community after ordination.

Clergy and Laity

It was the loss of the close community connection over the course of church history that led to an almost exclusive focus on the personal powers and rights that were conferred on those ordained. The ordained were distinguished from the laity by the powers that they received to consecrate the eucharist, forgive sins, and so on. The self-identity of the ordained was increasingly based on these powers rather than on their relationship to a local church that needed their ministry. Perhaps the zenith of this focus occurred in the twelfth and thirteenth centuries. The Third Lateran Council (1179) spoke of the community connection to ordination only in terms of whether the ordained priest had a bishop who would provide a proper living for him. Thus, at least in practice if not in theory, approval was given for ordination without any link to a community's ministry.

The Second Vatican Council promoted an increased awareness of the ministry of the laity and portrayed the church as primarily composed of the order of the faithful. Since the Council, the ministry of the ordained has been linked to the needs and mission of the order of the faithful. This has led to a gradual recovery of the connection between the ordained and the faith community they are called to serve.

Just as many members of the order of the faithful do not yet recognize their own ministry and their identity as people called to mission, so many have not yet grasped the shift in understanding of the role of the ordained within the church community. These two areas of understanding are intimately linked. The more clearly parishioners understand their own role in the church, the more clearly they understand the proper role of the clergy. The reverse is also true: The better people understand the proper function of the ordained, the better they understand their own role in the church and its mission. This highlights again the importance of helping the faithful understand holy orders more deeply, for it shapes their own identity in the church.

ENTERING AN ORDER

The term "ordination" itself reminds us that this sacrament celebrates the acceptance of new members into *orders* of service. The various ordained ministries are orders in the church, groups of people called and chosen for a specific ministry. One who is ordained joins that order, and in doing so, accepts responsibility for helping that order carry on its service to the larger church. Today we recognize three ordained ministries: the order of bishop, the order of presbyter (priest) and the order of deacon. All those who are ordained into one of those orders join a group already serving the church in a particular way. Ordination is not a personal privilege but a call to service. Being part of a particular order does confer certain powers and responsibilities; these are the means of serving the church community rather than the privileges of the ordained.

The initiation into an order is expressed ritually in each of the ordination rites. A bishop is ordained by at least three other bishops, who welcome him into the order of the episcopate. At the ordination of priests, after the bishop imposes hands on those being ordained, all the priests present also impose hands as a symbol of welcome to those joining their order. In a similar way, all deacons present at the ordination of deacons welcome their new brothers into their order with a sign of peace.

Seeing the ordained as members of various orders in the church can also help the laity recognize the significance of their own order, the order of the faithful. As for all orders in the church, joining the order of the faithful through baptism is a call and a commitment to being part of a group carrying on the mission of Christ. Much of the mission of the ordained is to help the faithful carry out their mission as the fundamental order of the church.

This renewed vision of the relationship between the ordained and the laity is essential to the ongoing renewal of the church itself. It requires careful balance that sees the importance of the ordained ministries without denigrating the ministry of the laity. The opposite also seems to occur sometimes today, with the ministry of the ordained being denigrated by some of the laity. The ordained do not need to be on a pedestal, yet their ministry is essential to the work of the church and needs to be respected and supported.

THE THREE ORDERS

Even though the name of the sacrament itself reminds us that it deals with more than one order, many people think of ordination as focused solely on presbyters (priests). It is important for all members of the church to understand the different orders of ordained ministry and their respective functions.

The order of bishops, also known as the order of the episcopate, derives its name from its function. The Greek word *episcopos* means overseer, and the task of the bishop is to oversee the work of the church as a whole, coordinating the various ministries in the diocese. In the rite of ordination, the new bishop is told, "As a steward of the mysteries of Christ in the church entrusted to you, be a faithful overseer and guardian. Since you are chosen by the Father to rule over his family, always be mindful of the Good Shepherd, who knows his sheep and is known by them and who did not hesitate to lay down his life for them" (*Ordination of Deacons, Priests and Bishops,* chapter 5, #18, in *The Rites of the Catholic Church,* vol. 2 [New York: Pueblo, 1980]; subsequent references are to this edition). Bishops also bear a collegial responsibility for the work of the entire church in union with the bishop of Rome, the pope: "Never forget that in the Catholic Church . . . you are incorporated into the college of bishops. You should therefore have a constant concern for all the churches. . . . Attend to the whole flock in which the Holy Spirit appoints you as an overseer of the church of God" (#18).

The name of the order of deacons also indicates the ministry of that order. The Greek *diakonein* means to serve, and deacons focus the community's ministry of service or charity. "As a deacon," the bishop tells them during their ordination rite, "you will serve Jesus Christ, who was known among his disciples as the one who served others. Do the will of God generously. Serve God and mankind in love and joy" (chapter 2, #14).

The role of the presbyter or priest, on the other hand, is not so clearly indicated in the name of the order. *Presbyter* in Greek means elder, which does not immediately suggest the ministry this order serves. The rite of ordination is also not very clear, suggesting primarily that the presbyter is a co-worker with the bishop and shares in the bishop's ministry. "Priests are co-workers of the order of bishops. They are joined to the bishops in the priestly office and are called to serve God's people" (chapter 3, #14). This makes sense in light of the history of the order of presbyter. Presbyters were originally the bishop's council of advisors, who began to function in the place of the bishop in outlying communities when the bishop could not be personally present. So the presbyter is like a bishop, but usually functions in one parish while the bishop functions in the whole diocese.

FORMATION FOR CELEBRATION

If a parish is going to celebrate an ordination of a priest or deacon at the parish itself, or if many parishioners will be going to the cathedral for the ordination of a parishioner or someone who has served the parish (for example, as a seminarian intern), good catechesis will help them to participate well in the celebration. The need is not so much for knowing the details of the rite, for the assembly's ritual role is not much different than in a Sunday Mass. But some familiarity with the unique elements of the ordination rite will be helpful.

What is most important, however, is having a healthy understanding of the role of the ordained minister and the importance of these orders in the life of the church. This will enable members of the assembly to give thanks to God for the gifts of these ministers and for their service to the church rather than focusing on the honor conferred on those ordained.

When the assembly is invited to give their consent to the choice of a deacon, a priest or a bishop, they should understand that they are being asked to affirm their sense that God has called these men to serve the church. The applause that often expresses this consent is probably less appropriate than the suggested response "Thanks be to God." Applause may suggest honoring the candidates rather than thanking God for calling them to serve the church. A sung acclamation of thanks or praise would be preferable.

The use of the Litany of the Saints before men are ordained as deacons, priests or bishops is a clear reminder of the importance of prayer for those ordained. Parishioners who do not attend an ordination might still be encouraged to pray this litany for those being ordained whenever holy orders is celebrated in the diocese.

Some reflection on the meaning of the laying on of hands may also help members of the assembly to appreciate the ordination rite. This ancient gesture of conferring office through the power of the Holy Spirit, followed by the prayer invoking that Spirit, is the central ritual action of holy orders.

Other rites that may warrant some reflection are the vesting with the appropriate vestments or symbols of office and the presentation of the book of the gospels (deacons and bishops) or of the chalice and paten (priests) as symbols of the ministry to which each order is called.

CONCLUSION

Providing adequate catechesis and formation for the celebration of the sacrament of holy orders is a significant pastoral challenge. Efforts made to help the faithful understand and appreciate this sacrament will bear fruit far beyond the sacrament itself. It will help the faithful understand the purpose of the ordained ministry, and this, in turn, should help them appreciate the purpose and dignity of their own order.

All the orders within the church today are called to work together to further the mission of Christ and prepare the way for the kingdom of God. The better that clergy and laity understand and value one another's ministries, the more effective the church will be in carrying out the mission entrusted to it by the Lord Jesus. May efforts to catechize the faithful about the meaning of this sacrament lead to such mutual understanding and support.

QUESTIONS FOR REFLECTION AND DISCUSSION

1. Have you ever taken part in an ordination Mass? If so, what do you remember about the celebration? If not, would you like to participate in such a celebration? Why or why not?

2. How would you explain the importance of this sacrament to the ongoing life of the church?

3. In the early church, priests and bishops were selected by the communities they would serve. What advantages and disadvantages can you see to such a system? Would you favor or oppose returning to this pattern? Why or why not?

4. How would you explain the purpose of each of the three orders: deacon, priest and bishop?

5. How would you describe the ministry of the order of the faithful? How do the orders of bishops, priests and deacons relate to this basic order of the church?

6. How could your diocese encourage all members of the church to celebrate the ordination of new ministers, even though only a small number could actually take part in the ordination Mass?

7. How could your parish help people to better understand the sacrament of holy orders?

8. How can we increase awareness of the responsibility of the whole church, clergy and lay, to nurture and call forth leaders for the future?

Chapter 6

Witnessing Love and Commitment: Liturgical Formation for Celebrating Marriage

Because liturgy can often seem disconnected from the everyday life of the people who gather for worship, the challenge for much of Catholic worship today is to integrate elements from the cultural life of the people into the liturgy.

When it comes to weddings, however, the opposite may be true. The cultural and social and commercial expectations and practices that shape people's image of a wedding are often diametrically opposed to the church's understanding of the sacrament of marriage and the ritual that celebrates it. This poses a difficult challenge for parish leaders who seek to form the faithful to celebrate the sacrament of marriage well.

Many Catholics assume that the culture's approach to a wedding and the church's approach should be the same. Their picture of the ideal wedding seems to be drawn from a combination of weddings they have seen on television (from soap opera weddings to the nuptials of Prince Charles and Princess Diana) and memories of weddings they have experienced over the years. The resulting image is often far removed from the liturgy that the church envisions for celebrating Christian marriage.

NOT A SPECTATOR SPORT

One of the most obvious differences between the popular view of a wedding and the church's liturgy is that the liturgy is not intended to be a spectator event. In the popular view, a wedding is seen as a production or a pageant, and the function of the "audience" is to watch and take pictures and be suitably impressed by the pageantry. The wedding is a showpiece, and the more elaborate and expensive, the better.

This is very different from good liturgy. The church sees a wedding as a celebration by the assembly of the love of God revealed in the love of two people God has brought together. It is neither a production nor a spectator event but a communal celebration of prayer and worship.

Yet when most Catholics gather for a wedding, they come together expecting to be spectators. Even when the assembly is composed largely of active Catholics, it is not uncommon that they stand or sit there with little or no participation in the action of the liturgy itself. The priest can say, "The Lord be with you," and the response is total silence. It is as though all the Catholics present have suddenly forgotten their role in the liturgy. They know the responses, of course, but often they seem to forget that they are supposed to be taking part in the action.

Starting Out Right

This mentality is reinforced, of course, by the way many weddings begin. Rather than the liturgical procession described in the Catholic ritual for marriage, the beginning of many weddings is more of a style show for the bridesmaids and the bride. With the groom and his attendants waiting up front, the female members of the wedding party come down the aisle like models on a fashion runway, complete with cameras flashing and background music. The bride comes last, accompanied by her father, who "gives her away." It is pomp and ceremony, but it is not liturgy.

The Catholic ritual, by contrast, begins with a liturgical procession. The acolytes and the priest or deacon enter first, followed by the wedding attendants (as couples) and the bride and groom with their parents. The procession, like almost all entrance processions for worship, is accompanied by the entrance song.

Here's how the entrance is described in the *Rite of Marriage:* "If there is a procession to the altar, the ministers go first, followed by the priest, and then the bride and bridegroom. According to local custom, they may be escorted by at least their parents and the two witnesses. Meanwhile, the entrance song is sung" (#20, in *The Rites of the Catholic Church* [New York: Pueblo, 1983]; subsequent citations are to this edition).

The importance of starting with a full liturgical procession can hardly be overstated. If the liturgy starts with the culture's focus on dresses and pictures, the "audience's" role as spectators is strongly reinforced and it is almost impossible to get them to become a liturgical assembly and to shift to proper participation in the liturgy.

This may be far more important than anything parish leaders can say to people about what the marriage liturgy should be. While catechesis is important, the way weddings are conducted in Catholic churches teaches far more effectively. What we do speaks more loudly than what we say.

A Communal Celebration

The participation of the whole assembly in the celebration of Christian marriage should flow from an understanding of the community's relationship to the couple being married. It is common in our culture to speak of the wedding as "the bride's day." The implication is that the bride should have complete control over what happens that day, since the wedding belongs to her. Leaving aside for the moment the sexist nature of such a statement, such a position is radically contrary to the nature of a sacrament as a celebration of the Christian community.

When a couple comes into the midst of the Christian community to celebrate their love and commitment, they are a focal point of the celebration but the liturgy still "belongs" to the community of faith. The community gathers around this couple to pray for them, to support their commitment and to witness their union. The wedding is supposed to be a community action around the couple. The faith community proclaims its beliefs and values in this celebration.

The Christian couple, in celebrating marriage in the community, is taking on a vocation within the church. Just as bishops, priests and deacons take on a vocation when they are ordained, a couple married in the church takes on a vocation to live out their baptisms in the married state. It is this commitment to live out their faith in union with one another that the community celebrates and affirms in the wedding.

Marriage Witnesses

Though canon law requires the presence of a priest and at least two witnesses for the celebration of a Catholic marriage, all those present for the celebration function as witnesses. They have gathered to celebrate the love of God revealed in this couple, and they witness and affirm the commitment of this bride and groom to one another for life.

This witness is supposed to be ritualized by a simple response that is commonly overlooked. After the couple has exchanged their vows, the minister says, "You have declared your consent before the Church. May the Lord in his goodness strengthen your consent and fill you both with his blessings. What God has joined, men must not divide" (#26). The assembly is supposed to respond at this point with an "Amen," but most often no response is heard. The ritual does not provide any clear cue for this response, and few people know that a response is expected. Perhaps it would be appropriate to sing a "Great Amen" at this point to highlight the assembly's witness of the couple's commitment. The presider might even chant these concluding lines to lead into a sung response.

It might well be argued that the Catholic marriage rite should include a fuller ritual action to express the community's role in the celebration. Until that day arrives, some catechesis of the faithful is needed to make this brief ritual response meaningful. The challenge is not simply to get them to say or sing the response but to recognize the importance of the assembly's witness and their affirmation of the couple's vows.

Beyond this simple ritual moment, those who plan weddings need a consistent focus on the assembly. The choice of music especially needs to be geared to fostering full participation by all those present. The preparation of a worship aid that includes the musical selections, or at least indicates where to find them in the hymnal, is a significant help. Verbal encouragement is also important, perhaps including a brief rehearsal before the wedding begins. Weddings almost always bring together people from various parishes and different denominations. Without considerable encouragement and practical support, many members of the assembly will be unable to participate. A rehearsal of the sung parts and comments that encourage participation remind everyone that the liturgy is not a stage production but a communal action in which all are to take part.

Understanding the role of the assembly in witnessing the couple's commitment might also prompt better efforts at involving the assembly in the vows themselves. Having the couple (and the wedding party) face the assembly for the questions before their vows reminds the assembly of their role. Making sure that the assembly can hear the couple as they exchange their vows is also important. Expecting couples to have the presence of mind to speak loudly enough for the assembly to hear might be unrealistic, but arranging a microphone to amplify their voices is usually not difficult.

BEYOND SUPERSTITION

Wedding days are often marked by various remnants from past ages. A number of customs have developed in various cultures that may not be appropriate today. Some of these are really superstitious elements that have no proper place in a Christian wedding. Where I live, for example, it is considered bad luck for the groom to see the bride on the wedding day before she comes down the aisle. This often prevents the bride and groom from welcoming their friends and family, a custom that can go a long way toward making people feel welcome and encouraging them to take part in the liturgy itself. This simple step of hospitality on the part of the bride and groom helps people move beyond the pageant mode that the superstition encourages.

Many people also consider it an omen of good luck to start the wedding on the half-hour so that the minute hand of the clock is rising as the wedding begins. (One wonders how long this one will last with the current prevalence of digital timepieces that have no clock hands!)

Catechesis is needed to help people move beyond such superficial and superstitious concerns. People need to recognize that such superstition is ultimately contrary to a faith that relies on the providence of a loving God rather than depending on luck. Challenging superstition really means inviting people to faith.

Other Dated Customs

Other common customs are not superstitious but may still be inappropriate today. One is the tradition that the father of the bride "gives her away." Even the wording of that phrase ought to ring warning bells in the minds of contemporary women. The custom comes from the time when the bride was seen as the property of her father until she was "sold" and handed over to become the property of the groom. The custom hardly seems appropriate in an age of gender equality.

Beyond its origins, the focus on the father of the bride alone also seems inappropriate ritually. The mother of the bride and the parents of the groom have had just as large a role in the formation of the couple who are being married. All four parents ought to be included in the entrance procession, as the Catholic ritual assumes. (The convoluted relationships that arise in our culture from divorce and remarriage may require some careful discernment as to which parents and stepparents should be included in the procession, of course.) This also would help us move away from the idea that the wedding belongs to the bride alone, that this is her day. At the very least, the day belongs to the bride *and* the groom. Gender equality must go both directions.

Another ancient custom is throwing rice on the couple as they leave the church. This derives from an ancient pagan fertility ritual, which seems somewhat out of place at a Christian celebration. Moreover, it often creates a mess and is not healthy for birds who feast on the discarded rice. Other substitutes may have their own problems—bird seed thrown instead of rice can create just as big a mess; helium balloons are also harmful to birds who ingest them; soap bubbles are innocuous but not a very rich symbol. Perhaps parishes could develop a custom of guests raising their hands over the bride and groom as they leave the church and speaking or chanting a simple blessing of the couple.

BROAD-BASED CATECHESIS

Marriage preparation with the prospective bride and groom offers good opportunities to address many of these issues with them. Once they understand the background of traditional customs, many couples are quite willing to embrace a more Christian approach to celebrating their wedding. With extended catechesis, they also come to see the wedding as a time for their family and friends and other members of the Christian community to actively participate in the celebration of their love and commitment.

Catechizing the couple is not enough, however. The whole faith community needs to update its understanding of Christian marriage and how it should be celebrated. This will require consistent catechesis over a long period of time. Though most Catholics have embraced the reforms of the liturgy mandated by the Second

Vatican Council, many have not yet included weddings in their renewed understanding of worship as an action of the whole community gathered together.

The community's role becomes clearer when weddings are celebrated during Sunday Mass, and such celebrations are an effective way to form a parish for this sacrament. The regular Sunday prayers and readings are used, although one of the readings may be replaced by one from the wedding list. The rest of the elements of the wedding liturgy are celebrated at the usual times in the Mass, but it is clear that the Mass belongs to the whole assembly and that all are expected to participate in the worship. Many parishes have experienced this, often with the marriage of a couple who is active in parish ministry. The practice may well become more common in the years ahead as the number of priests continues to decline and separate weddings with Mass become less available. Experiencing weddings at Sunday Mass enhances the communal nature of a sacrament often seen as private.

Raising the assembly's awareness of the community's role is key to the whole effort of formation for celebrating the sacrament well. All the sacraments are communal worship. They all presume and require an assembly that understands its role and is willing to join together to create a prayerful experience. Only when every member of the assembly knows and accepts his or her role in creating a good wedding liturgy will this sacramental moment be all that it can be. We may never reach that point, of course, but solid and consistent catechesis over an extended time can move us much closer to it than we are today.

QUESTIONS FOR REFLECTION AND DISCUSSION

1. What differences do you see between the popular view of weddings and the church's understanding of the celebration of the sacrament of marriage?

2. What images or experiences have shaped your own expectations about weddings? How would you describe your expectations?

3. Recall your wedding or one you attended recently. What made it prayerful? What distracted from prayer and worship? What helped or hindered the assembly's participation in the liturgy?

4. Weddings sometimes begin in different ways. What beginnings have you observed? Did some seem to lead you more easily to prayer and worship?

5. Have you been to weddings where most people fully partici-
    pated in the worship? Have you been to some where few took
    part? What made the difference?

6. What customs or superstitions about weddings are common
    where you live? Which ones could find a proper home in a
    Catholic wedding?

7. What effect has your participation in weddings (of other peo-
    ple) had on your own commitment to your marriage or other
    relationships in your life?

8. What approach to catechizing the parish do you think would be
    most effective in your own community?

9. Have you ever experienced a wedding at a regular Sunday Mass? If so, describe your reactions. If not, how do you think you would respond if you did?